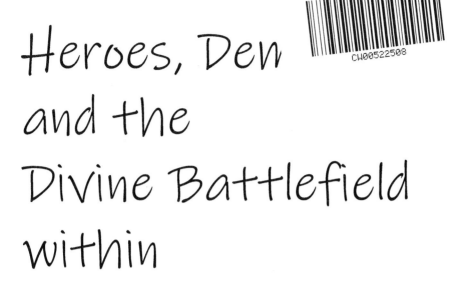

Heroes, Den and the Divine Battlefield within

Winning our inner battles with the help of the ancient wisdom of the Bhagavad Gita

Earth

Namaste

Coaching, mentoring, teaching - sharing whatever little nuggets of knowledge I have picked up has been a vital part of my life over the past 30 years – whether it was back in medical school or in various roles since.

This book is a motley collection of my reflections and musings about this beautiful journey we are on.

Simple, heartfelt- or as we say in Hindi- **"Dil se"** -
"from the heart".

Contents

Book of Life

Heroes, Demons and the Divine Battlefield within

The Sacred Flame

Guardian of the Sacred Flame

Code 652

Weeds of the Past

Mother and Son

Boat & the Ship

What If?

The Divine Battlefield...(part II) Arjuna's burden

Who is the Expert?

The Paradox

The Storm Within

The Journey of Eight Steps...part I

The Journey of Eight Steps...part II

The Journey of Eight Steps...part III

The Red Silk Scarf

One Health

Life is too short

What are we forgetting?

Book of Life

We have already won the lottery of life. Our earth, as far as

we are aware, amongst billions and billions of planets, is the only

one that has the right conditions where life has evolved and

thrived. Think of the odds.

Add to that the odds of when you were conceived. The pairing of

chromosomes, the crossover of certain specific parts - millions of

recombination possibilities- but it was you who was born, having

beaten and won these astronomical odds of existence.

That makes you special.

You have won the gift of this most amazing and beautiful book

of life.

Who knows how many chapters there are in our individual books.

Some chapters take our breath away; some leave us struggling

to breathe.

Some, we want to go on forever, some we can't wait to finish.

And it is one's own journey. One's own book.

Not a competition, definitely not a race to come first.

You read it at your own pace.

You read and complete the chapters.

Whether the ones that give you joy or the ones full of pain and grief.

You read, complete and move on to the next chapter.

Some are a breeze, some arduous and difficult to finish.

But never despair.

Always remember they can be completed, closed and you can move forward.

Often, it is just about finding that strength and courage in you.

Heroes, Demons and the Divine Battlefield within

The Bhagavad Gita (often also referred to as The Gita) has been a companion since childhood. It has been a source of strength, solace and comfort when I have lost a loved one. And it has been there to steady me when I have had self-doubts and loss of confidence.

For fellow travelers reading this book who may not have come across this scripture I will give a very brief introduction.

Mahabharata (Maha-bharata) and Ramayana (Ram-aya-na) are the two major Sanskrit epics of ancient India.
The Bhagavad Gita forms part of the Mahabharata that is dated to the second century BCE (Before Common Era).

It is a discourse between the warrior prince Arjuna and Lord Incarnate - Krishna on the battlefield -Kurukshetra (Kuruk-shay-tra)- where the two opposing armies are facing each other ready for battle - and Arjuna (arguably the greatest warrior of all time and an archer beyond compare) is gripped with fear and self-doubt.

There is so much I have learnt (and am learning) from this great epic.
Two key messages for here -

First -the transient, fleeting nature of our time on this earth, in this body versus the immortality of the soul
(I compare it to the relentless march of our Genes).

Second- the topic of this chapter- that - the Kurukshetra (Kuruk-shay-tra)- or the divine battlefield as I like to call it is within each of us. Inside us.

Each of us is Arjuna.
Each fighting.
Each day to win that battle between the good and the evil forces, between the Heroes and the Demons.

And just as the triumphs of yesterday don't assure one of victory in the upcoming battles, past losses (countless those might be), or even ones suffered today, do not condemn one to future defeats.

And, Devi, The Indian Goddess also reminds us that the battle is within.

Which army are we willing on to win?

Which army are we feeding? Which one are we providing the weaponry?

Who will triumph?

And you may have realised by now - that choice- as to who wins- is also somehow strangely within.

So what does The Gita tell me.

That it is alright to be faced with self-doubt. It is alright to be concerned with what the outcome of one's endeavors will be. But let that just be transitory.

Have faith in your ability. Let belief run through your veins.

For remember the Hero is within.

The army equipped and ready to battle is within.

The Triumph is WITHIN

And that choice who wins is DEFINITELY within.

(This chapter is based on what The Bhagavad Gita's message means for me. This is not intended to be a commentary on the Holy Scripture).

The Sacred Flame

Have Respect for the Self.

Have Compassion for the Self.

Love for the Self

Love for your journey. Respect for your journey

Reflection from the Original Source

Call it God, Parmatman (Par-maat-ma), the energy from the Big

Bang.

Whatever entity you identify with.

It energises you.[1]

It gives you awareness.

It makes you aware of the environment- being able to respond

to changes in the environment.

It burns bright in you.

It is the Sacred Flame in you.

Further reading

[1] Sri Sri Paramahansa Yogananda, God Talks with Arjuna: The Bhagavad
Gita. Royal Science of God-Realization, 2007

Guardian of the Sacred Flame

Look inside.

Create self-awareness.

Realise your worth.

The sacred flame that burns inside you, inside that temple.

Protect it.

Guard it zealously.

Guard that sacred space and be mindful of who you let into that sacred temple.

Realisation of self-worth leads to confidence.

We have so many different roles in our lives. So many threads intertwined.

Distant friends, close friends, work colleagues, family, close relatives, partner, spouse, children, grandchildren.

The more self-aware you are, more confident you will be in giving yourself fully to those roles.

The more you are aware of the Self, the more you know your identity, the more comfortable you will be in different environments.

The less scared you will be of losing your identity.

Realise your worth. Be kind to yourself.
Fill the cup of your soul with confidence.
Fill it with love and kindness.
You can't give what you don't have.

Love the Self.
Guard that flame passionately.
Guard that sacred space.
Do not speak low of it.
Do not speak low of yourself.

Code 652

Weekday mornings in our household, during school term time, are probably not too different from many a household.

A few cycles of alarm-snooze-alarm, groggily getting out of bed, putting the kettle on, tea and then a mad rush to get ready - ensuring all three of us (my wife, son and I) have had breakfast, and ensuring our son does not miss his school bus.

For the morning schedule to go smoothly he is expected to be out of his bed latest by 6:40 a.m.

A few years ago, on one such day, imagine my shock, when after getting ready I found my then 9-year old still in his bed, fast asleep. Time 6:52 a.m. !!

Which meant he would be late in getting ready, with barely any time to have the hot breakfast I had planned and just about make it to the bus stop or worse miss his bus.

I lost my cool, calling him out loudly, with my voice raised, to wake up and get out of bed. He woke up gingerly, eyes groggy and now even more disoriented by his father shouting loud instructions from the doorway.

At that moment it suddenly dawned as to what was I really doing.

My impatience, my loud voice probably an attempt to turn the clock back to at least 6:40.

Well forget 12 minutes, time wasn't going to turn back for even
a nanosecond. It wasn't even going to pause for a nanosecond !!
That event had already happened, and I had no control over it.
My actions were only making the situation worse.
I could however influence what would happen in the next 20 odd
minutes.
Probably not enough time for him to have a proper hot
breakfast, but I could definitely put together something quick
and easy for him to eat before leaving for school.

And that has become in our household what we call Code 652.
When one of us is fretting and fuming about something that has
already happened and nothing can be done, the others call out
"Code 652"!

And isn't that true about so many situations in life. We worry,
fret, feel guilty about something that unfortunately might have
happened but is now in the past.

Rather than worrying about the past, why not focus our energy in a positive manner on something that we CAN do, have some control over.

Time moves relentlessly in one direction. The arrow pointing forward, straight ahead.

Calls not returned, emails left un-replied, relationships gone cold, for whatever reason.

I am not here to say cast a blanket of forgiveness.

All I am saying is that has now happened.

You can't turn the arrow of time.

You can't do something to change that event or that moment.

But you CAN definitely do something now.

So, call out your code.

Stop worrying and getting sucked in by the negative energy of that black hole.

Rather, focus and channelise your positive energy on what can be done.

And ask What is it that I can do?

P.S. – In case you were wondering, my son did have his breakfast (different one to the original I had planned) and made it in time for his school bus.

Weeds of the Past

The past is gone
Yes, learn from the errors and mistakes but do not let them
define who you are.

Errors, mistakes – yes
Regrets – No.

Every time you visit the past you empower it.
Like watering a weed full of spikes.
It grows, encroaches upon and takes over some of your present.

Precious, invaluable present.
Which will slip by like sand through a fist.
Very soon Today will be a memory. Gone. FOR EVER.
You decide what you write on that page.
Only memories will survive. And even they will fade away.

Own it.
Own the Past. Close those chapters.
Closing, letting go does not mean erasing.
It means no longer spending time and energy on the past.
Forgive & that starts with Forgiving yourself.

That requires Courage.

And that sits deep inside you. Find it.

Move forward.

It is Your Journey.

Mother and Son

"When this 'I' shall die, then will I know who am I."
- Hindu scriptures[1]

We often say, " I don't have an ego". "I have no problem with my ego". "It is not about the ego."
Be it with our spouse, partner, children, parents, relatives, in-laws, friends, neighbours, work colleagues.
Countless interactions, some easy, some not.
Some difficult, some leaving us worse for wear !!

And when that little voice inside us says "was it your Ego?", we snap back, "of course, not!! I don't have an ego."
But then again and again, sometimes exhaustingly so, we find ourselves having difficult interactions, some of which we so dearly would want to be pleasant ones.
And that retort again, "but I don't have an ego."
"No, no, no...it is not about the ego!!" "there's no ego involved"
Sounds familiar.

I would like you to think of it in a slightly different way.

Let's go way, way back and start at the very beginning – the Source - you can call it God, Energy from the Big Bang or whatever else you like.

Now, there are two manifestations of this - [1]
1. Spiritual or Consciousness being one.
2. The other being the matter and everything in it.

So, the Consciousness on one side, the physical & sensory manifestation on the other side.

Where does Ego come in you might ask here?

The Consciousness gets differentiated to become eight intelligences[1].
Two key ones to note here –
   1. The Universal Spirit
   2. The Reflected Spirit

Reflected spirit is nothing but in essence the reflection of the Universal Spirit, and it energises the objects on which it falls.

This leads to an awareness for the object of its own entity.

This is important- **"aware of its own entity"**.

In other words, **Self-awareness or Self-consciousness.**

This Self-consciousness- is the Ego [1].

Progeny of Consciousness.

Mother and Son.

You could also think of the process as the changing relationship between parent & child.

The child receives the parents' reflection.

Grows and develops intelligence, self-awareness and becomes an individual in their own right.

"I don't have an ego". Or "Should I not have an ego".

What is more relevant here is Ego "is". It exists.

The important thing is where is the focus?

Ego is principled when focused inward on the self.
But has faults when focused outward and entwined with
material desires.

"Material" in material desires needn't be money i.e., financial
desires. It could be anything — physical, mental, emotional.

Remember that battle from chapter 2. That battle has to be
fought countless times, every day to keep the focus inward and
prevent the Ego from being entrapped by the outward pulls
exerted by material desires.

Not easy!! But a battle that has to be fought and won.

Further reading
[1] Sri Sri Paramahansa Yogananda, God Talks with Arjuna: The Bhagavad
Gita. Royal Science of God-Realization, 2007

Boat & the Ship

Visualise two men living next door to each other in a village by the sea.
Let's name the village – "Self on-sea".

Both have identical resources.
Both build identical boats and take them out to the sea.
A beautiful calm day and they are enjoying their sea trip.
However, soon the weather changes for the worse. Waves crash against the two boats and both suffer identical damage.
Somehow, they make it back to the shore.

One of them learns from the experience and focusses on fixing the boat, how to make it stronger. Uses the resources he has and makes a bigger stronger boat.
The other one blames the weather, the waves and just about repairs his boat to make it sea-worthy.
Round 2 - again both boats go out on the sea.
Boat 1 suffers some damage, but less so.
Boat 2 suffers same damage as before.
Back on shore the former gets about learning from his experience and makes a bigger, better, stronger boat.

The latter again blames the weather, the sea, the waves - no learning.

Just about fixes the boat, not realising that the damage is now starting to seep into the planks.

I would like you to run this scenario in your mind for a few more rounds.

And you end up with - on one side a big, strong ship; it's captain confident in its strengths and focused on learning and self-improvement.

Each day, every day- learning and self-improvement.

On the other side, we see a small, weak rickety boat where the captain kept blaming the external influences- the waves, the sea, everything except himself. His ego preventing him from focusing on the self.

No self-awareness, no improvement.

So, what do you want to be?

The one who is focused on the self; on the time, resources, efforts spent on building the strong hull, and confident in its strength.

Or someone focused on the waves.

The ocean same.
The waves same
Crashing against two structures.

One confident, calm.
Other not so. Restless. Caught in a whirlpool, with an ego, not turned inward on self-awareness but enslaved by ignorance, arrogance and entrapped in blaming the external waves.

Where you focus, where you put your energy - **that choice is Definitely Yours.**

What If?

What if I lose?

You will have gained valuable experience to take forward to future battles.

What if I win?

The plaudits are yours to enjoy. You still would have gained valuable experience to take forward to future battles.

The battlefield awaits you.
That's Karm (action).

Your right is to the effort, not to the fruits thereof.
The key message from The Bhagavad Gita

Do not be put off by the scale of the task.
Increase your effort because that's what you can control.

The Divine Battlefield...(part II)
Arjuna's burden

Remember Arjuna, the mighty warrior from Chapter 2.

Also, recall it is you who is metaphorically Arjuna fighting that battle every day, on that divine Battlefield within.

Is it not true that so often we find ourselves in battles which we probably did not want to be part of, would have done everything in our power to avoid; we simply end up in them as life events to which we have to react to. Not us being thrust in battles, but rather battles thrust on us, at our doorstep. (Alert - we need to be careful here and ensure we do not start victimising ourselves).

And you probably find yourself asking the questions that I so often find myself pondering

Did Arjuna instigate the battle?

Did Arjuna instigate the events that led to that battle?

Did Arjuna want that battle?

The answer- probably No.

And also, more often than not we end up carrying the burden of some of those losses and heavy defeats for years and decades - whole lifetimes.

I want you to pause and reflect here and spend a few moments taking stock of those battles.

So, when there were countless defeats, when you suffered body blows, when you fell bloodied, battered, bruised and broken, and getting up seemed impossible. And when the whole world, your world seemed like it had given up on you. And the fight had taken huge chunks of your physical, mental, emotional, spiritual (and probably financial) health.

You found that inner steel and you stood up.

You did - to take on the new battles.

To fight another day.

Is it then right to keep carrying that burden and keep blaming the Arjuna inside of you?

Is it not then fair, to also step back, and every so often give yourself, your grit, your courage, and your strength to overcome those losses some credit?

And when you turn around and glance at the past battles fought on that Divine battlefield won't you also see some big triumphs? Huge sacrifices were probably required but you fought on and triumphed.

Give yourself credit for those too. You absolutely have earned that right.

For it is the defeats and the triumphs that come together in the sacred fire to forge the warrior that is you.

The mighty Arjuna on the Divine Battlefield within.

Who is the Expert?

Who is the expert?

Who knows your life journey best?

Who is the coach of your team?

Then why are you waiting for others' opinion as to whom to select on your team.

Take Ownership.

Own your Sacred Space

Own your Time

Own your past

Own your Present & the Future

Own this Journey

Your Journey

All of this of course requires Courage

You have the Courage

All you need is to believe in Yourself.

The Paradox

Take ownership.

It is your journey.

Events of the past have happened and gone.

Stop carrying that burden.

Let it go.

Learn from it.

But do not mistake 'carrying the burden' with learning.

"It is my responsibility to learn"

"I do not want to make that mistake again."

Fair enough, but use it as a learning, to light the path ahead.
Not as a heavy backpack filled with rubble & stones; the heavy
burden that is slowing you down on your journey.

Carrying the burden is exhausting, nerve wracking and worse
slowing you down on this beautiful journey of life.

But it requires strength and courage to let go of that burden.

To make the past your own.

No one else to share those losses with.

To own those defeats requires real strength.

But remember past losses do not condemn you to future defeats on this divine battlefield.

It requires strength to own the past.

It requires strength to put that heavy backpack down.

It requires strength to Stop and Introspect.

On this Journey with a destination, but no end.

The Paradox.

Mistakes, errors - Yes. Regrets No.

One life - that is whizzing past.

Days become weeks, then months, then years.

Soon decades have passed you by.

All in the blink of an eye.

How long are you planning on carrying the burden?

Embrace the past.

With authority.

Own it.

The Storm Within

Followers of the Hindu scripture -The Ramayana may recall the story of the 'Kasturi' deer. A musk deer obsessively searching for the fragrance, little realising it arose from within.

The story of Elsa from the Disney movie Frozen probably slightly different but with a similar message.

The storm raging within.

Isn't that what we find ourselves doing so often? Searching, running, trying to tame external storms, totally oblivious, ignorant, or worse - deliberately choosing to ignore the fact that the restlessness is raging all the while within us.

Change the camera angle.

Focus inwards. Create self-awareness.

Muster the strength to calm those storms raging within.

Not easy. Requires strength, forgiveness and the resolve to go into the eye of the storm and control it.

Take courage- you have with you, your mighty army on the Divine battlefield within, ready, awaiting your clarion call to take on the demon forces.

And once again, the choice who wins is DEFINITELY within you.

The Journey of Eight Steps...part I

Introspection
Identifying the Self
Recognising the Self
Locating the Self
Awareness of the Self
Self-awareness
Self-Control
Calmness

Introspection – That honest conversation with Self

The key word being Honest

All you need to ask yourself and answer – Am I being truthful with myself?

The first step on that journey begins with Introspection.

And that beautiful journey will only begin when you take that first step.

And to have that conversation requires Courage.

We spend so much time and effort in knowing others. Spending quality time and resources in knowing, understanding others.

Why not for ourselves?

Why not that effort spent in knowing the Self?

That introspection will lead to a better understanding of the Self- Identifying it, Recognising it and Locating it.

So many of us go through our lifetime not even knowing what our true Self is? where our true Self is?

Identification, recognition, & location of the Self will lead to an Awareness of the Self's needs and wants.

All the time being guided by that honest, impartial introspection.

Keep doing that- on repeat – and it leads to Self-awareness.

You truly and supremely become aware of the Self.

That leads to Self-control.

And finally, Calmness.

No matter what the external situation, what others are saying or doing, you manage your inner Calmness.

True, Strong, Unwavering Focus on the Self.

The Journey of Eight Steps...part II

AS if the journey wasn't difficult enough, Six Demon Kings –
each a ferocious warrior, each fiercer than the other will be on
that journey of yours as well.

1. Anger

2. Greed

3. Lust

4. Delusion

5. Pride

6. Envy

They have immense power. Power to control you and prevent
you from completing your Journey.

But the warrior in you also has equal power, weapon
for weapon, to control them.

And who controls whom...

That CHOICE is within YOU

The Journey of Eight Steps...part III

No matter how difficult the journey, no matter how steep the climb, no matter who wants to control you and prevent you from reaching your destination, you have the COURAGE, the STRENGTH and the RESOLVE in you to not only complete this beautiful journey but also enjoy it.

You just need to Believe in yourself

FOCUS on the SELF
FOCUS on the NOW

The Red Silk Scarf

One of the commonest phrases that comes up in the
conversations I have with my coachees-
"I put expectations on them".
Probably all of us have done that and felt let down when people
don't meet those expectations.
Let's just read that sentence again & slowly
I. Put. Expectations. On. Them

So often we hold onto things, events and people so hard.
Expect so much and then get upset, angry and resentful when
they can't meet those expectations that we place on them.

Say, I invite you for an evening tea to my place.
We have a great time. Two friends, reminiscing about old times,
enjoying each other's company; the time together filled with
heartfelt joy, laughter and happiness.
Then I bring and place on your shoulder this exquisitely beautiful
red silk scarf. It is amazingly pretty. Soft silk, handwoven with
beautiful motifs.
But what I didn't know beforehand was you can't take it.

Now that could be due to a myriad of reasons. You don't like it, you don't want it from me, you don't need it, you don't fully comprehend the beauty or "value" or worse you get an allergic reaction by that material.

That then makes me resentful and changes the tone of the otherwise lovely conversation.
So, you see where I am going.

I put something on you.
I put expectations on you.
I. Put. Expectations. On. You
You cannot meet them
I feel resentful

Why not just appreciate and enjoy the moment? Fully immersed in that moment in time and space without judgements.

Why do those moments have to have an add-on or even worse be tainted by the burden of those expectations.
Why does that time and space have to bring in its embrace a "return on the investment" you made?

Why do we so often not fully appreciate, and with gratitude, the beauty of that moment - the smiles, the laughs, the happiness that it has brought to our hearts.

"It is not easy". "it is easier said than done".
I hear you say. Of course, it is not easy. That is why we are having this conversation. That is why it is probably one of the commonest string of words that comes up in my conversations with my coachees.

Of course, we will have expectations of people. We are social beings, we like to be in the company of others, interact with others. The pandemic has brutally shown us that.

Self-awareness does not mean putting up walls or becoming an isolated, lonely island.
Far from it. What I am saying is rather than making it about "them", "they didn't do this", or "they did this", why not focus your efforts on what YOU are doing.

Either don't "burden" them with that expectation.
Or don't let that expectation come in the way of fully enjoying each other's company.

Focus that camera angle on the self.
Work on changing what you can.
Be that change.

One Health

Look after yourself.

As I see it there are five components of health

Physical

Mental

Emotional

Spiritual and yes...

Financial (too)

Balance all five

Set time aside for the Self. Take Ownership. Nourish it

Start with Breathing. Try this exercise

    Inhale for a count of 4

    Hold for a count of 4

    Exhale for a count of 4

Try it. Gentle. Repeat.   Let that life breath fill your lungs.

        Inhale – Patience

        Hold- Self

        Exhale – Gratitude

Life is too short

Life is too short.

But is it?

I came across this quote the other day.

"it isn't that life's too short.

By the time we realise it's worth and start valuing it, it is time to turn back."

Think about it.

Start living.

Start loving.

Start valuing

Your life

Your "Self"

What are we forgetting?

Or avoiding thinking about

The occurrence of which is a fact
Probably the only one guaranteed fact in the future.

Then why live as if it is never going to happen.
Why live as if there's an endless supply of days at our disposal.

Yesterday is gone. FOR EVER.
Today will be gone very soon.
Yes, a lot may not have happened (or not happening) as you would have wanted.

But then, a lot (and probably more) must also have happened as you would have wanted.

And, a lot of great, positive things, relationships, friendships, work achievements might have happened that you had probably not even dreamt of.

Why not cherish every passing day.

Why not fill our days with positivity.

Why not fill our days with gratitude.

Why not LIVE every day?

Printed in Great Britain
by Amazon